UNDERSTANDING
-------- OUR --------
MUSCLES

LUCY BEEVOR

capstone

Edited by Brenda Haugen
Designed by Russell Griesmer and Jennifer Bergstrom
Original illustrations © Capstone Global Library Limited 2016
Picture research by Jo Miller
Production by Jennifer Bergstrom
Originated by Capstone Global Library Limited

21 20 19 18 17
10 9 8 7 6 5 4 3 2

Library of Congress Cataloging-in-Publication Data
Names: Beevor, Lucy, author.
Title: Understanding our muscles / by Lucy Beevor.
Description: North Mankato, Minnesota : Capstone Press, [2017] | Series:
   Raintree perspectives. Brains, body, bones! | Audience: Ages 8-11. |
   Audience: Grades 4 to 6. | Includes bibliographical references and index.
Identifiers: LCCN 2016036102|
ISBN 9781410985811 (library binding) |
ISBN 9781410985859 (paperback) |
ISBN 9781410985972 (eBook PDF)
Subjects: LCSH: Organs (Anatomy)—Juvenile literature. | Human
   biology—Juvenile literature. | Human anatomy—Juvenile literature.
Classification: LCC QM27 .B44 2017 | DDC 611—dc23
LC record available at https://lccn.loc.gov/2016036102

Acknowledgements
We would like to thank the following for permission to reproduce photographs: Capstone Studio:
Karon Dubke, 5, 13, 15; Getty Images: Corbis Historical/Richard Bergman, 12; Newscom: Blend Images/
ERproductions Ltd, 26; Redferns via Getty Images/Amy T. Zielinski, 24; Shutterstock: Air Images, 27,
Alila Medical Media, 21, baranq, 25, BioMedical, 10, design36, 9, 29, DM7, cover, Nerthuz, 19, sciencepics,
8, Sebastian Kaulitzki, 7, 11, 22, stihii, 14, Tefi, 16-17; design elements: Shutterstock: designelements,
Natasha Pankina, Ohn Mar, PILart, Studio_G

Every effort has been made to contact copyright holders of material reproduced in this book. Any omissions will be rectified in subsequent printings if notice is given to the publisher.

Printed and bound in the USA
062017   010618RP

TABLE OF CONTENTS

YOUR ACTIVE BODY

Imagine you are playing in a basketball tournament, and the final seconds are counting down. Your team needs one point to win. The crowd cheers as you jump up and throw the ball toward the basket. You score! During all the action, you probably didn't even think about your muscles. But around 640 muscles kicked in to make the play a success. It's a great moment for your basketball team. But it was your muscle team that made it happen.

If your body were a machine, your muscles would be the engine. A car engine uses the energy in gasoline to turn the wheels. Your muscles take the energy from the food you eat and use it to power all of the movements you make.

See for Yourself

If you want to know what muscle feels like, grab some raw beef or chicken. Be sure to wash your hands afterward! The meat we eat is animal muscle.

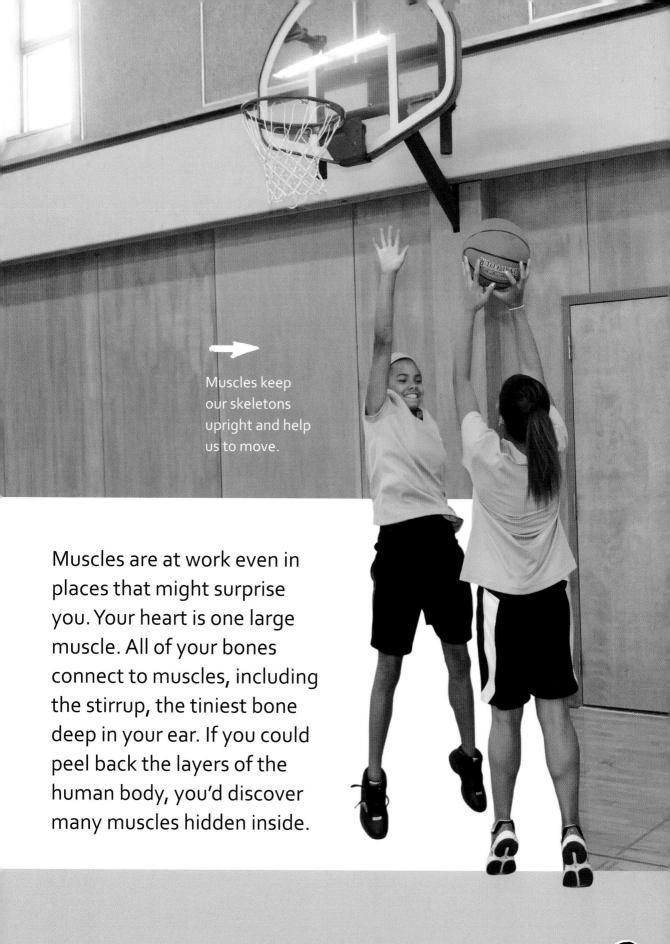

Muscles are at work even in places that might surprise you. Your heart is one large muscle. All of your bones connect to muscles, including the stirrup, the tiniest bone deep in your ear. If you could peel back the layers of the human body, you'd discover many muscles hidden inside.

GETTING UNDER YOUR SKIN

Imagine that you could wiggle out of your skin and look at what remains. The first thing you might notice is that you are all red. Dark-red muscles cover your body from head to toe.

But muscles don't just wrap around you like a blanket. Your muscles cover you in layers. They also come in whatever shape it takes to get the job done. Long, thin muscles move your arms and legs. Your stomach is lined with flat, rectangular muscles. The muscle that wraps around your shoulder is shaped like a triangle. And when you stick out your tongue, you use the round muscle that circles your mouth and muscles that change the shape of your tongue.

See for Yourself

Tiny muscles surround every hair on your skin. When you're cold, the muscles tighten to push the hairs up, causing goose bumps.

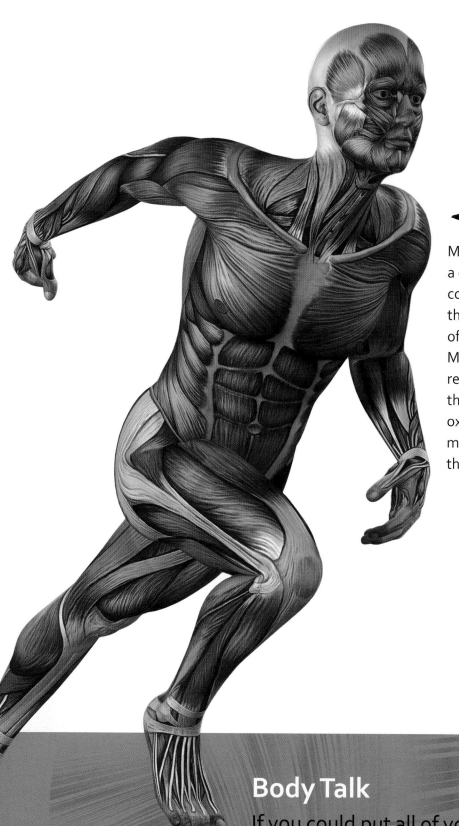

Muscles are mostly a deep red-brown color because they contain lots of myoglobin. Myoglobin is a reddish protein that delivers oxygen to the muscles to keep them working.

Body Talk

If you could put all of your muscles on a scale, they would equal about half of your total body weight.

More than Meets the Eye

If you look at a muscle under a microscope, you will see long, skinny **cells** called **muscle fibers**. Muscle fibers are easily damaged, so small groups are bundled together to make them stronger. Many bundles of muscle fibers make up one muscle.

There are two types of muscle fibers in the body. Fast-twitch fibers **contract** quickly but tire easily. Slow-twitch fibers contract slowly but are able to keep going for longer. Most muscles in the body contain both types of fibers.

Fast-twitch muscle fibers are useful for quick bursts of energy, such as jumping to catch a ball or sprinting to class. Slow-twitch muscle fibres are useful for longer activities, such as hiking or long-distance running.

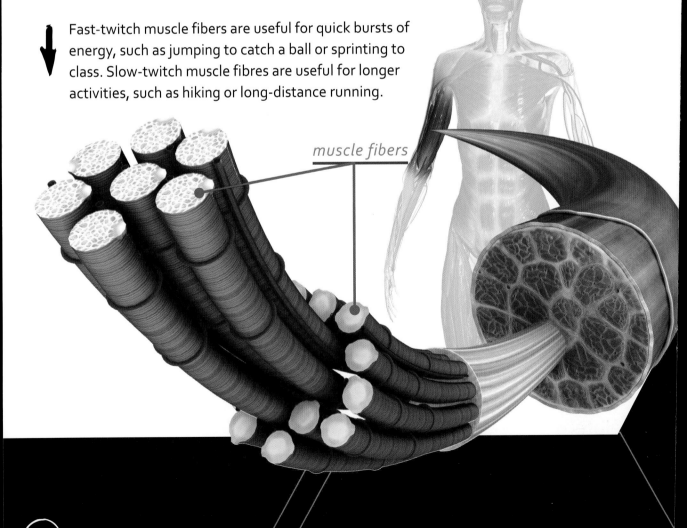

muscle fibers

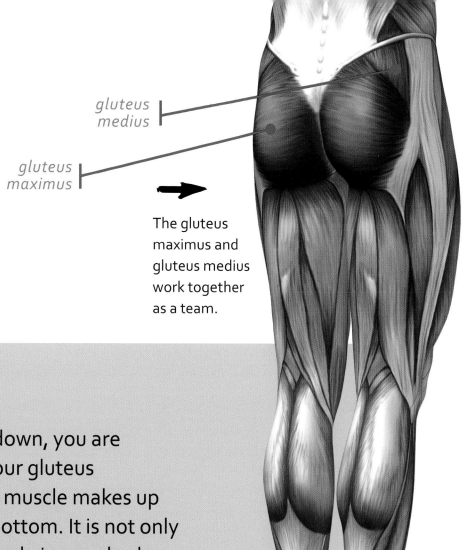

gluteus medius

gluteus maximus

The gluteus maximus and gluteus medius work together as a team.

Sit on It!

When you sit down, you are perching on your gluteus maximus. This muscle makes up most of your bottom. It is not only the largest muscle in your body but also one of the strongest. The gluteus maximus connects your upper legs to the bones at the base of your spine. It works hard when your hip needs power, like when you climb stairs. If you could lift it up and look underneath, you would find the gluteus medius. This muscle works alongside the gluteus maximus to help you walk, run, and jump.

Hold on Tight

Muscles couldn't do much work if they were flopping loose in your body. They need to be connected to bones. *Tendons* are thick bands of tissue that connect the muscles to your skeleton. Your calf muscle attaches in three places. One tendon attaches to your foot. Two more tendons attach to your thighbone. The muscle in the arch of your foot has five tendons. One tendon connects to your heel bone. The other four tendons connect to your four smallest toes.

Most tendons are tough, rope-like bundles of fiber, while some are flat sheets.

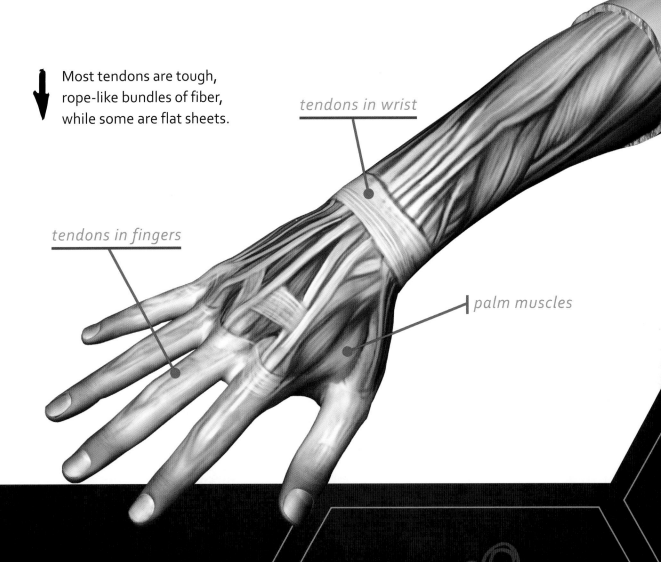

tendons in wrist

tendons in fingers

palm muscles

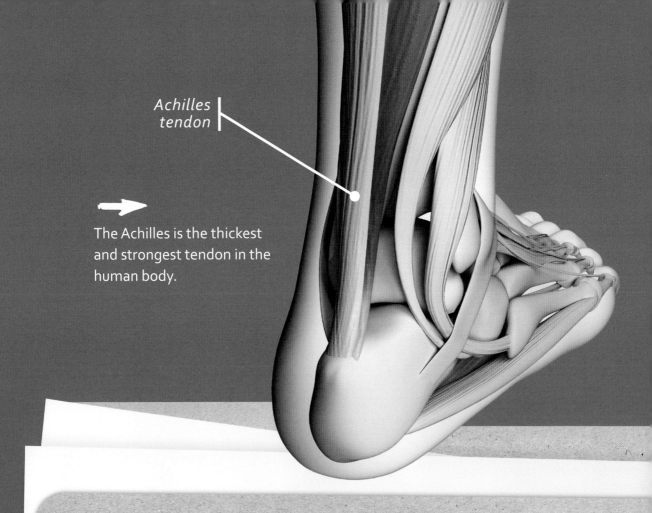

*Achilles
tendon*

→

The Achilles is the thickest
and strongest tendon in the
human body.

See for Yourself

Ball your hand into a fist, and look at the inside of your wrist.
You can see and feel your tendons through your skin. You
can also feel the Achilles tendon at the back of your ankle.
This tendon is named after a story about a Greek god named
Achilles. According to the story, Achilles died when a poisoned
arrow hit him in the heel. If you tear your Achilles tendon,
you will need surgery before you can walk again.

Body Talk

There are no muscles in the fingers, only ligaments, tendons,
and bones. The muscles in the palm and forearm pull the
tendons in the fingers, which cause the fingers to move.

GET A MOVE ON

Even though they come in various shapes and sizes, the muscles underneath your skin are all called skeletal muscles. These muscles attach to your skeleton, and their job is to move your bones.

Bones and muscles are shaped to work together. If you look closely at a bone, you will see hollows and grooves. These markings show where tendons were attached. Bone experts can tell how strong a person was by looking at the size of those marks. Strong muscles leave deep grooves in the bone.

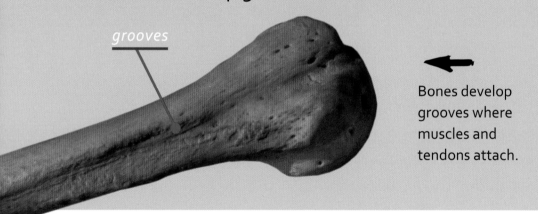

grooves

Bones develop grooves where muscles and tendons attach.

Back in Action

Your back muscles allow you to move in many directions. You can reach up to shoot a ball at a basket. You can bend forward to grab a Frisbee off the ground. You can twist sideways or lean backward to pass a note to the person behind you. Lots of muscles work together to make these movements. These muscles attach to the different segments of your spine, which bend and flex depending on the movement.

It takes more effort to frown, so keep smiling. It's far less work for your face muscles.

See for Yourself

Some face muscles attach to skin. Take a look in a mirror, and smile. Did you know it takes 17 face muscles to create your smile? Now frown. Your face uses 43 muscles to do this!

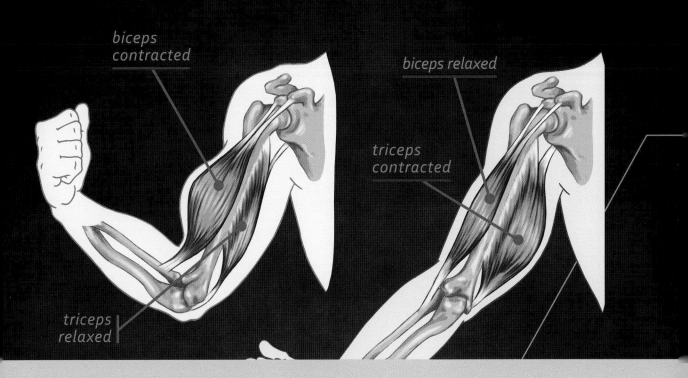

biceps contracted

biceps relaxed

triceps contracted

triceps relaxed

An early scientist thought that the biceps "bump" looked like a mouse under the skin. He named it a "muscle," using the Latin word "mus," which means "little mouse."

Working Together

Skeletal muscles move the body by pulling on bones. Each muscle can get shorter, or contract, by itself. But a muscle can't stretch back out unless another one pulls on it. When you bend your arm, your biceps muscle contracts. This pulls your forearm up. At the same time, the triceps muscle at the back of your arm relaxes. To straighten your arm again, the triceps muscle contracts, which relaxes the biceps. All muscles have at least one partner that pulls in the opposite direction in this way.

Team Players

Most movements require a full team of muscles. When you take a step, the muscles in your legs are working hard. But other muscles pitch in too. The muscles of your ankles, hips, stomach, and back all work to keep you upright as you walk.

You can strengthen your biceps muscles by lifting small weights or doing chin-ups.

See for Yourself

When people say "show me your muscles," they usually want you to bend your arm. This is one of the easiest ways to see a muscle team in action. Watch your upper arm as you bend at the elbow and clench your fist. Do you see your biceps rise up? Now straighten your arm and you'll see the triceps tighten and the biceps drop. The two muscles are working together to move your forearm up and down.

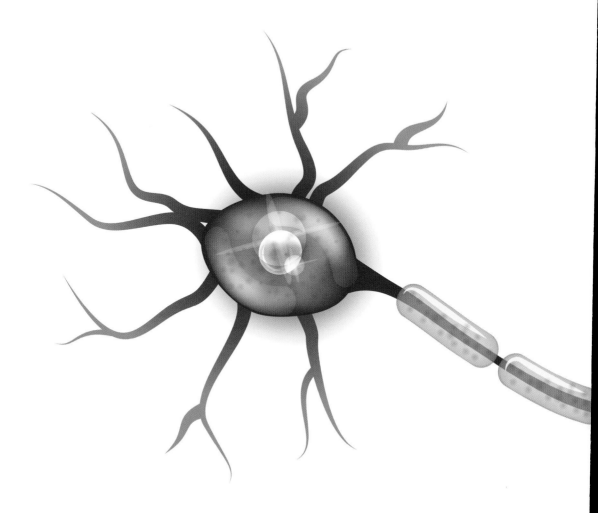

A Shrinking Solution

When you do a karate kick, muscles all over your body contract. But how do muscles actually get smaller? The action starts all the way down in the muscle fibers. Tiny threads of **protein** normally lie end to end inside muscle fibers. To contract, the threads slide together and lie side by side. When they do, the muscle fiber gets shorter and fatter.

The Body's Messengers

Nerves connect to muscle fibers. They constantly send thousands of messages from your brain to your muscles. When you make a large movement, such as jumping, your brain sends a message to your nerves. The nerves then tell lots of muscle fibers to contract. When you make small, careful movements, your nerves only set a few muscle fibers in motion.

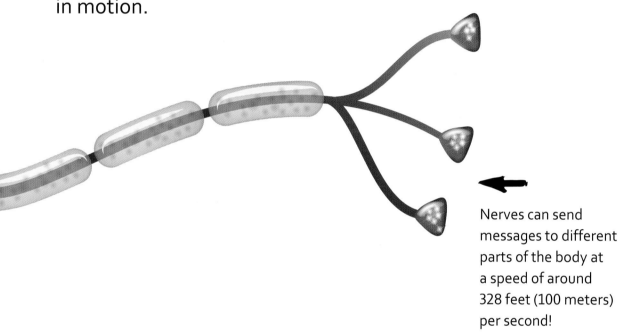

Nerves can send messages to different parts of the body at a speed of around 328 feet (100 meters) per second!

Body Talk

There are billions of nerve cells, known as *neurons*, in the human body. The number of neurons in a human brain alone is an amazing 100 billion. If they were lined up end to end, they would form a line 600 miles (965 kilometers) long. That's about the same distance as from New York City to Cincinnati, Ohio!

DEEP DOWN INSIDE

If you could peer deep into the body, you would find more muscles. These muscles don't connect to bones, and you can't see them move. They are the *involuntary* muscles that power your *internal* organs.

Always Working

You don't have to do much to give involuntary muscles a workout. They are always busy. Your stomach muscles break down your food. They also help you to throw up when you get sick. Muscles work hard in your intestines, lungs, and bladder too. Muscles even line your *blood vessels*. They control which parts of the body get the most blood. When you run a race, they send more blood to your legs. When you eat, they send more blood to your stomach.

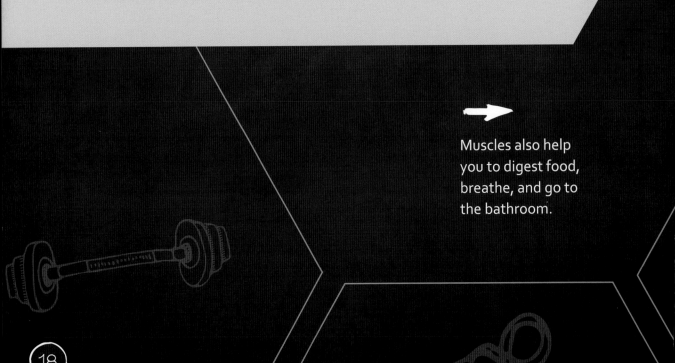

→ Muscles also help you to digest food, breathe, and go to the bathroom.

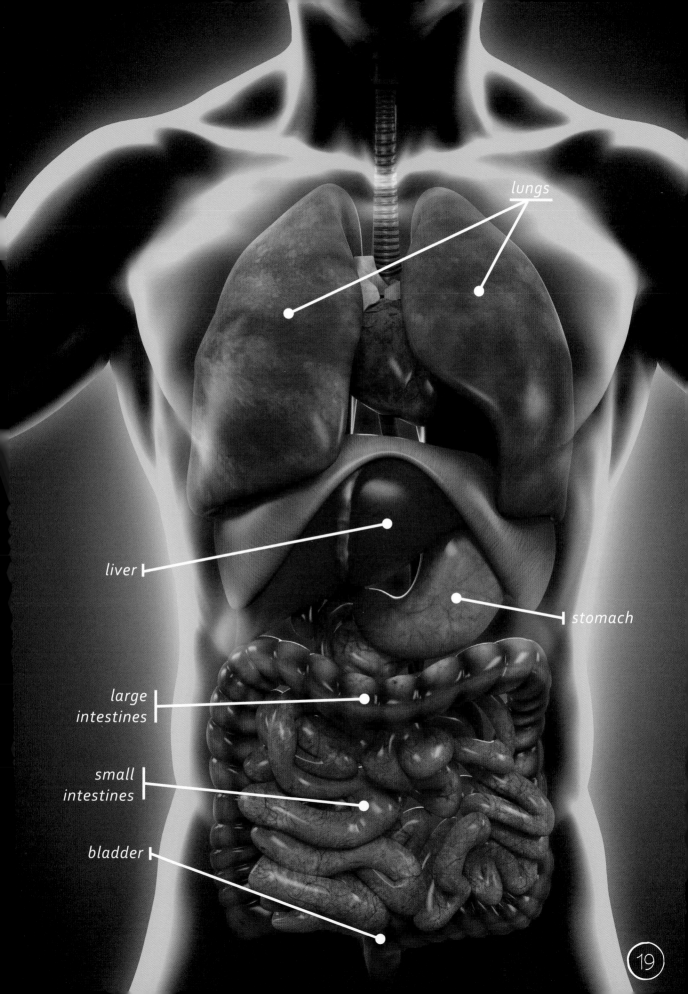

lungs

liver

stomach

large
intestines

small
intestines

bladder

In a Heartbeat

Your heart is one of the strongest muscles in your body. It is the only part of your body that is made of cardiac muscle. This muscle has been beating night and day since before you were born. Your heart beats between 60 and 90 times each minute. When you exercise or get scared, it beats much faster.

Pump It Up

The heart works like a pump. First it fills up with blood. Then the muscles contract, and blood gushes into the blood vessels. Each pump sends out 0.75 cup (59 milliliters) of blood. But you have about 20 cups (4.7 liters) of blood in your body. No wonder the heart has to work so hard! The muscles contract over and over to keep your blood moving.

Your heart is a special pump. The left and right atriums fill with the blood returning to the heart from the body. The left and right ventricles pump the blood back out to the body through the blood vessels. This process is called circulation.

Body Talk

All of your blood passes through your heart once each minute. When you're doing hard exercise, it can travel through your heart in just 15 seconds.

The Beat Goes On

Before the heart muscle relaxes, two valves snap shut. They keep blood from leaking backward into the heart. When the valves close, they make a "lub-dub" sound. Doctors can tell if your heart is healthy by listening to that sound through a **stethoscope**.

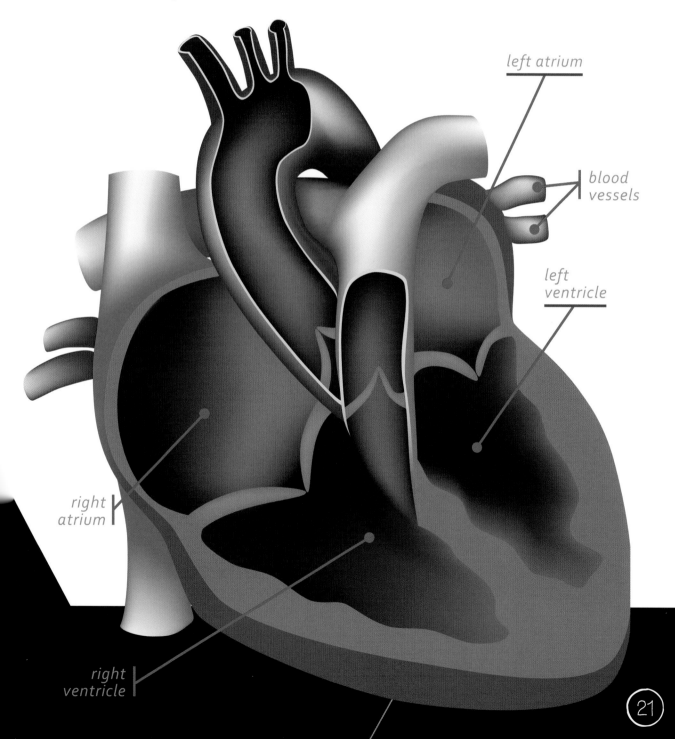

left atrium

blood vessels

left ventricle

right atrium

right ventricle

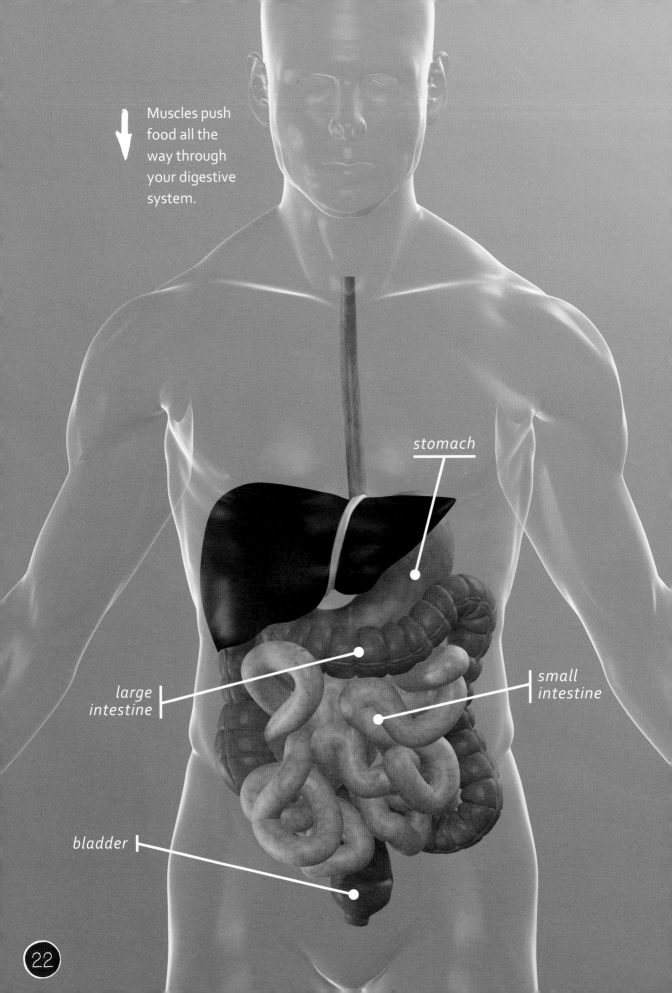

Muscles push food all the way through your digestive system.

stomach

large intestine

small intestine

bladder

Moving Out

Imagine squeezing all of the toothpaste out of a tube. You would start from the bottom and then squeeze higher and higher until you reached the top. The muscles in your *digestive system* work the same way. They squeeze one small section after another to move the food along. When you swallow a spoonful of breakfast cereal, it travels from your mouth to your stomach. Then it moves through your intestines and finally out of your body.

Hold It!

The bladder is the body's storage tank for urine. The walls of the bladder are made of involuntary muscle. These muscles can stretch to hold over 4 cups (0.9 liters) of urine. When the bladder is holding about 2 cups (0.5 liters), the muscles contract, and you feel the urge to go to the bathroom. But at the base of the bladder, there is a muscle you control. When you decide to relax this muscle, the urine comes out.

MUSCLE POWER

Playing a sport such as basketball helps your body to get stronger. As you run around the court, your involuntary muscles send more blood to your legs. If you put your legs to work regularly, your muscle fibers will grow thicker and stronger.

Regular exercise helps all of your muscles to work better. Your heart gets better at pumping, and you will be able to run longer without getting tired. Exercise even helps keep the muscles in your digestive system working well.

 English classical pianist James Bartlett put his muscle memory to the test when he won a Young Musician of the Year competition in 2014, when he was 18 years old.

See for Yourself

Our muscles can also become stronger in another way. When we practice an action over and over again, such as playing the piano or catching a ball, we can get *muscle memory*. The muscles "remember" how to perform the action, so they know what to do the next time. They get better each time they're called to action. Practice makes perfect.

Lifting heavy weights takes many years of special training with the right equipment and professional coaches. Don't try this at home!

Body Talk

The smallest skeletal muscle in the human body is the stapedius. It moves the body's tiniest bone—the stapes, or stirrup—inside your ear. The muscle is about the size of this dash (-).

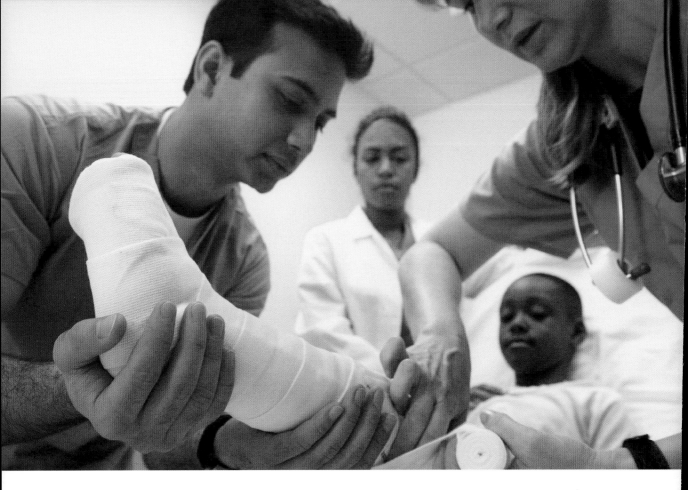

Use It or Lose It

If you don't use your muscles, they get smaller and weaker. When you have a broken leg, the doctor puts it in a cast to keep it from moving. The cast lets the bone heal, but you can't use your leg muscles. When the cast comes off, the leg that was broken will be much thinner and weaker than the other leg. This is because the muscles didn't have any work to do while the bone was in the cast. You need to exercise that leg to make the muscles strong again.

 Exercising your muscles will keep them in top condition and help to prevent injuries.

Make Your Move

Start your engines! Your body is one powerful machine. You can perform a cartwheel in the school gym. You can curl into a ball and roll down a hill. Or you can suck a strand of spaghetti into your mouth. From your head to your toes, muscles always keep your body on the move.

People are born with all the muscle fibers they'll ever have. Muscles don't just grow by themselves. The only way they can get bigger is with exercise.

SEE INSIDE:
MUSCLES

A — **EYE** The muscles of your eye move more than 100,000 times every day.

B — **DELTOIDS** The deltoid muscles of your shoulders help you to raise your arm and rotate it in all directions.

C — **PECTORALS** Without the pectoral muscles of your chest, you wouldn't be able to cross your arms or breathe properly.

D — **ABDOMINALS** Your abdominal muscles are sometimes called a "six-pack" because each muscle bulges in three places on both the left and right side.

E — **QUADRICEPS** The quadriceps femoris is actually a group of four leg muscles that stretch out your knee.

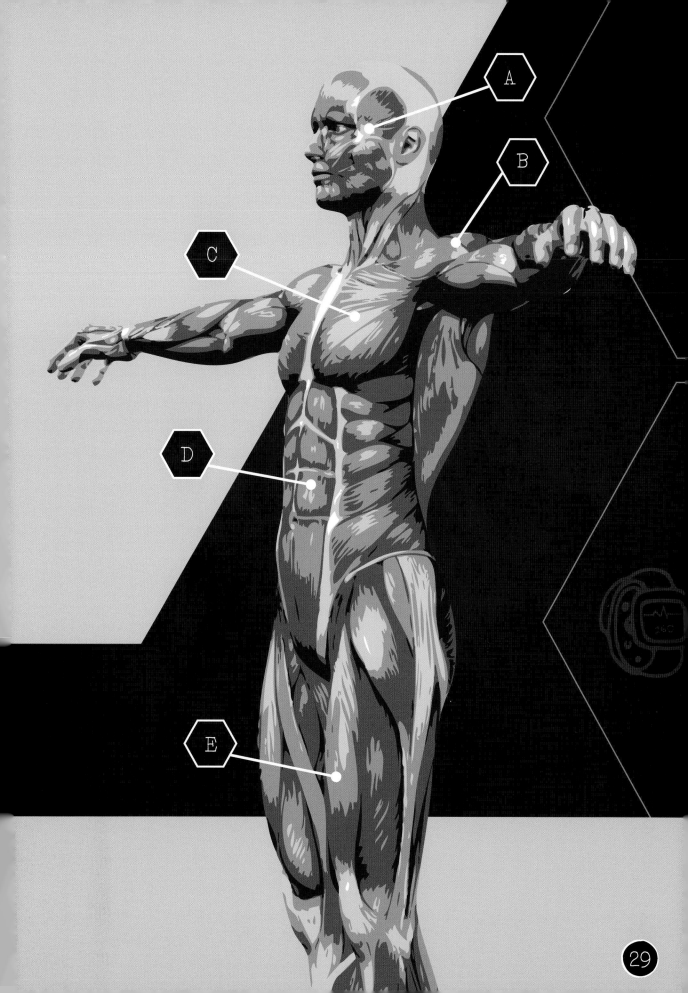

GLOSSARY

blood vessel (BLUHD VE-suhl)—tube that carries blood through your body; arteries and veins are blood vessels

cell (SEL)—smallest structure in the body; different types of cells do different jobs

contract (kuhn-TRAKT)—tighten and get shorter by squeezing in toward the middle

digestive system (dye-JESS-tiv SISS-tuhm)—group of organs responsible for breaking down food into energy for the body and getting rid of waste

internal (in-TUR-nuhl)—inside the body

involuntary (in-VOL-uhn-tehr-ee)—done without a person's control

muscle fiber (MUSS-uhl FYE-bur)—long, thin cell made of many long proteins

muscle memory (MUSS-uhl MEH-mor-ee)—ability to repeat a movement exactly, without thinking

nerve (NURV)—thin fiber that sends messages between your brain and other parts of your body

neuron (NOO-rahn)—special type of cell that transmits signals to the body

protein (PROH-teen)—type of molecule that helps the body to function

stethoscope (STETH-uh-skohp)—medical tool used by doctors and nurses to listen to the sounds of a patient's heart, lungs, and other areas

tendon (TEN-duhn)—strong band of tissue that attaches a muscle to a bone

READ MORE

Brown, Carron, and Rachael Saunders. *The Human Body.* Shine-a-Light. Tulsa, Okla.: Kane Miller Books, 2016.

Martin, Bobi. *The Muscles in Your Body.* New York: Britannica Publishing, 2015.

Wilsdon, Christina, Patricia Daniels, and Jen Agresta. *Ultimate Body-Pedia.* Washington D.C.: National Geographic Kids, 2014.

INTERNET SITES

FactHound offers a safe, fun way to find Internet sites related to this book. All of the sites on FactHound have been researched by our staff.

Here's all you do:

Visit *www.facthound.com*

Type in this code: 9781410985811

 Check out projects, games and lots more at
www.capstonekids.com

INDEX